This notebook belongs to

Juliette Bravo.
Love P&W
Happy birthday
X

Hi,
Congratulations on getting this book! You will love it!
Nice to meet you - I'm Bex Beltran.
I'm a superfan of journals, workbooks and notebooks and I hope you are too!
I'm also a podcast host, coach and teacher.
You can find out more about what I create and offer at http://bexb.org/
You can listen to the podcast, Release Your Resistance, wherever you usually listen to podcasts.

Shop other journals, workbooks and notebooks and get more info at http://bexb.org/shopjournals

Follow me socially at @bex_beltran

Copyright Beltran Creative Services LLC. All rights reserved. No part of this publication may be reproduced, distributed, or transmitted in any form or by any means, including photocopying, recording, or other electronic or mechanical methods, without the prior written permission of the publisher, except in the case of brief quotations embodied in critical reviews and certain other noncommercial uses permitted by copyright law.

Just 3 things.
For just 3 minutes a day.

Edit 3 items in 3 minutes.. every day for 99 days - by the end of this notebook you'll have gotten rid of close to 300 things!

Every day, check this notebook for a prompt with an area of your home or life to edit. Set the timer on your phone for 3 minutes.

In that time, choose 3 items from that space to THROW AWAY (it's also fine if you donate or use up these items).

Make a quick note of what you get rid of so you can see if there are any patterns or reminders to help you as you make decisions about what new things to bring into your space.

Keep track of ALL. THE. THINGS. you're editing out.

You'll be so PROUD of yourself and your progress!

Day 1

Date:

Take 3 minutes and look around your clothes.
Be on the lookout for: socks

Do you have a pair that always slip down and drive you crazy when you walk?
What 3 things can you throw out, donate, regift and get rid of?

1.

2.

3.

Realizations:

Notes/Reminders:

Day 2

Date:

Take 3 minutes and look around the bathroom.
Be on the lookout for: under sink area
Any old cleaning supplies? Any extras that can be donated?

What 3 things can you throw out, donate, regift and get rid of?

1.

2.

3.

Realizations:

Notes/Reminders:

Day 3

Date:

Take 3 minutes and look around the office. Be on the lookout for: junk mail

Unwanted correspondence and advertising?

What 3 pieces can you get rid of?

1.

2.

3.

Realizations:

Notes/Reminders:

Day 4

Date:

Take 3 minutes and look around the closet.
Be on the lookout for: undies

Any old shapewear or "special occasion" stuff you really don't want or need?

What 3 things can you get rid of?

1.

2.

3.

Realizations:

Notes/Reminders:

Day 5

Date:

Take 3 minutes and look around the office. Be on the lookout for: electronics & cords

Any old phones laying around?

What 3 things can you throw out, donate, regift and get rid of?

1.

2.

3.

Realizations:

Notes/Reminders:

Day 6

Date:

Take 3 minutes and look around the kitchen. Be on the lookout for: dishes

Any weird one-off dishes you never use?

What 3 things can you throw out, donate, regift and get rid of?

1.

2.

3.

Realizations:

Notes/Reminders:

Day 7

Date:

Take 3 minutes and look around the dressing area. .

Be on the lookout for: jewelry

Is there a necklace that always tangles? What 3 things can you throw out, donate, regift and get rid of?

1.

2.

3.

Realizations:

Notes/Reminders:

Day 8

Date:

Take 3 minutes and look around the office.
Be on the lookout for: hobby supplies

Did you ever buy a kit thinking you would do it, then never did?

What 3 things can you throw out, donate, regift and get rid of?

1.

2.

3.

Realizations:

Notes/Reminders:

Day 9

Date:

Take 3 minutes and look around the closet. Be on the lookout for: shoes

Do you have a pair that kills your feet?

What 3 things can you throw out, donate, regift and get rid of?

1.

2.

3.

Realizations:

Notes/Reminders:

Day 10

Date:

Take 3 minutes and look around the office.
Be on the lookout for: books

Do you have any coffee table books that are just collecting dust?
What 3 things can you throw out, donate, regift and get rid of?

1.

2.

3.

Realizations:

Notes/Reminders:

Day 11

Date:

Take 3 minutes and look around the bathroom or hall closet.

Be on the lookout for: linens

    Do you NEED all the towels in here?

 Is there anything that has seen better days?

What 3 things can you throw out, donate, regift and get rid of?

1.

2.

3.

Realizations:

Notes/Reminders:

Day 12

Date:

Take 3 minutes and look around the closet.
Be on the lookout for: accessories

Gloves with holes in the fingers?
A hat you'd never be caught in public wearing!
What 3 things can you throw out, donate, regift and get rid of?

1.

2.

3.

Realizations:

Notes/Reminders:

Day 13

Date:

Take 3 minutes and look around your digital universe.

Be on the lookout for: apps on your phone

What apps did you download and never start using?

What 3 things can you delete?

1.

2.

3.

Realizations:

Notes/Reminders:

Day 14

Date:

Take 3 minutes and look around the closet.
Be on the lookout for: clothes

Look for something that just isn't your style.

What 3 things can you throw out, donate, regift and get rid of?

1.

2.

3.

Realizations:

Notes/Reminders:

Day 15

Date:

Take 3 minutes and look around **Wild Card.**

Be on the lookout for: decor items

Wander through your space to see what decor items just aren't doing it for you anymore? What 3 things can you throw out, donate, regift and get rid of?

1.

2.

3.

Realizations:

Notes/Reminders:

Day 16

Date:

Take 3 minutes and look around your digital space.

Be on the lookout for: Docs in a Drive

Do you have slide presentations or pdfs that you never need to see again?

What 3 things can you move to the trash?

1.

2.

3.

Realizations:

Notes/Reminders:

Day 17

Date:

Take 3 minutes and look around the kitchen. Be on the lookout inside the drawers.

What serving and cooking utensils do you have duplicates of?

What 3 things can you throw out, donate, regift and get rid of?

1.

2.

3.

Realizations:

Notes/Reminders:

Day 18

Date:

Take 3 minutes and look around the kitchen. Be on the lookout for: food in the fridge

What's expired?

What 3 things can you throw out and get rid of?

1.

2.

3.

Realizations:

Notes/Reminders:

Day 19

Date:

Take 3 minutes. Look around your digital world.

Be on the lookout for: Friends you Follow

    Are there any "influencers" under whose influence you no longer want to be?

What 3 accounts can you unfollow, block or delete?

1.

2.

3.

Realizations:

Notes/Reminders:

Day 20

Date:

Take 3 minutes and look around the bathroom. Be on the lookout for: skincare

You bought it, but don't like it- now's the time to toss it!

What 3 things can you throw out?

1.

2.

3.

Realizations:

Notes/Reminders:

Day 21

Date:

Take 3 minutes and look around storage areas. Be on the lookout for: nostalgia

You don't need those decor items you bought 5-10 years ago!

What 3 things can you throw out, donate, regift and get rid of?

1.

2.

3.

Realizations:

Notes/Reminders:

Day 22

Date:

Take 3 minutes and look around the office.
Be on the lookout for: office supplies

Toss all the pens that don't work.

What 3 things can you throw out, donate, regift and get rid of?

1.

2.

3.

Realizations:

Notes/Reminders:

Day 23

Date:

Take 3 minutes and look around the bathroom. Be on the lookout for: other self care items

Look in the shower - what else can go?
What don't you need in here anymore?

What 3 things can you throw out?

1.

2.

3.

Realizations:

Notes/Reminders:

Day 24

Date:

Take 3 minutes and look around **Wild Card.** Be on the lookout in your outside area.

Any old flower pots or welcome mats that you don't need anymore?

What 3 things can you throw out, donate, regift and get rid of?

1.

2.

3.

Realizations:

Notes/Reminders:

Day 25

Date:

Take 3 minutes and look around your devices. Check the photos in your camera roll?

Have you kept any "utility" photos? Like a picture of a label or instructions that you don't need?

What 3 things can you throw out, donate, regift and get rid of?

1.

2.

3.

Realizations:

Notes/Reminders:

Day 26

Date:

Take 3 minutes and look around the closet.
Be on the lookout for: PJs

What was a gift, that isn't really you?

What 3 things can you throw out, donate, regift and get rid of?

1.

2.

3.

Realizations:

Notes/Reminders:

Day 27

Date:

Take 3 minutes and look around the kitchen. Be on the lookout for: spices

What would you even use this in?

What 3 things can you throw out, donate, regift and get rid of?

1.

2.

3.

Realizations:

Notes/Reminders:

Day 28

Date:

Take 3 minutes and look around the kitchen. Be on the lookout for: stuff in the cupboards

Lids with no containers?

What 3 things can you throw out, donate, regift and get rid of?

1.

2.

3.

Realizations:

Notes/Reminders:

Day 29

Date:

Take 3 minutes and look around your banking app or online bank account..

Be on the lookout for: Subscriptions

What are you spending $$$ on that you can cancel all together?

What 3 things can you cancel, suspend or pause?

1.

2.

3.

Realizations:

Notes/Reminders:

Day 30

Date:

Take 3 minutes and look around your storage. Be on the lookout for: travel stuff

What suitcases or bags have seen better days?

What 3 things can you throw out, donate, regift and get rid of?

1.

2.

3.

Realizations:

Notes/Reminders:

Day 31

Date:

Take 3 minutes and look around more storage areas.

Be on the lookout for: out of season stuff

Things from last season (or before) that were a good idea at the time, but didn't get used?

What 3 things can you throw out, donate, regift and get rid of?

1.

2.

3.

Realizations:

Notes/Reminders:

Day 32

Date:

Take 3 minutes and look around the closet.
Be on the lookout for: workout wear

What's just too worn to keep?
What did you buy that you thought you would love, but you really don't?
What 3 things can you throw out, donate, regift and get rid of?

1.

2.

3.

Realizations:

Notes/Reminders:

Day 33

Date:

Take 3 minutes and look around **Wild Card**.
Look around!

Any space, any place.. just find 3 items that no longer belong here!
What 3 things can you throw out, donate, regift and get rid of?

1.

2.

3.

Realizations:

Notes/Reminders:

Day 34

Date:

Take 3 minutes and look around the closet.
Be on the lookout for: socks

Any socks missing a mate?

What 3 things can you throw out, donate, regift and get rid of?

1.

2.

3.

Realizations:

Notes/Reminders:

Day 35

Date:

Take 3 minutes and look around the bathroom. Check through the under sink area

Any old partly-used products you forgot you had?

What 3 things can you throw out, donate, regift and get rid of?

1.

2.

3.

Realizations:

Notes/Reminders:

Day 36

Date:

Take 3 minutes and look around the office.
Be on the lookout for: papers

Is there information you're holding on to that's also available online?

What 3 things can you throw out, donate, regift and get rid of?

1.

2.

3.

Realizations:

Notes/Reminders:

Day 37

Date:

Take 3 minutes and look around the closet.
Be on the lookout for: undies

Is there a bra that doesn't show up well under things?

What 3 things can you throw out, donate, regift and get rid of?

1.

2.

3.

Realizations:

Notes/Reminders:

Day 38

Date:

Take 3 minutes and look around the office. Be on the lookout for: electronics & cords

Any chargers that don't charge anything?

What 3 things can you throw out, donate, regift and get rid of?

1.

2.

3.

Realizations:

Notes/Reminders:

Day 39

Date:

Take 3 minutes and look around the kitchen. Be on the lookout for: drinkware

Any cups you never drink out of?

What 3 things can you throw out, donate, regift and get rid of?

1.

2.

3.

Realizations:

Notes/Reminders:

Day 40

Date:

Take 3 minutes and look around the dressing area.

Be on the lookout for: jewelry

    Do you have that one metal piece that was cute, but now it's tarnished?

What 3 things can you throw out, donate, regift and get rid of?

1.

2.

3.

Realizations:

Notes/Reminders:

Day 41

Date:

Take 3 minutes and look around the office.
Be on the lookout for: hobby supplies

Did you get high hopes for a project, but it's not meant to be?

What 3 things can you throw out, donate, regift and get rid of?

1.

2.

3.

Realizations:

Notes/Reminders:

Day 42

Date:

Take 3 minutes and look around the closet.

Be on the lookout for: shoes

    Do you have a pair that's too worn out?

Any crazy shoes.. that you would really never wear (again)?

What 3 things can you throw out, donate, regift and get rid of?

1.

2.

3.

Realizations:

Notes/Reminders:

Day 43

Date:

Take 3 minutes and look around the office.
Be on the lookout for: books

Any old textbooks still haunting your shelves?

What 3 things can you throw out, donate, regift and get rid of?

1.

2.

3.

Realizations:

Notes/Reminders:

Day 44

Date:

Take 3 minutes and look around the bathroom or hall closet.

Be on the lookout for: sheets

Any sheets you don't use?
What 3 things can you throw out, donate, regift and get rid of?

1.

2.

3.

Realizations:

Notes/Reminders:

Day 45

Date:

Take 3 minutes and look around the closet or coat rack.

Be on the lookout for: accessories

The scarf that was a gift.. and not your style? What 3 things can you throw out, donate, regift and get rid of?

1.

2.

3.

Realizations:

Notes/Reminders:

Day 46

Date:

Take 3 minutes and look around your devices. Be on the lookout for: apps on your phone

What apps did you used to love.. but now you use a different app instead? Delete them all!

What 3 things can you get rid of?

1.

2.

3.

Realizations:

Notes/Reminders:

Day 47

Date:

Take 3 minutes and look around the closet. Be on the lookout for: clothing items

Find something that doesn't fit right. Do you have anything that is stained or damaged? What 3 things can you throw out, donate, regift and get rid of?

1.

2.

3.

Realizations:

Notes/Reminders:

Day 48

Date:

Take 3 minutes and look around **Wild Card.**

Be on the lookout for: soft goods

Which pillows are just blah?

What 3 things can you throw out, donate, regift and get rid of?

1.

2.

3.

Realizations:

Notes/Reminders:

Day 49

Date:

Take 3 minutes and look around your computer..

Be on the lookout for: Docs in Drive
Old assignments or projects you don't need anymore? any old lists or plans that are finished?

What 3 things can you get rid of?

1.

2.

3.

Realizations:

Notes/Reminders:

Day 50

Date:

Take 3 minutes and look around the kitchen.

Be on the lookout inside your drawers

Do you have a catchall drawer in your kitchen-

There are 3 things in there that can go

FOR SURE!

What 3 things can you throw out, donate, regift and get rid of?

1.

2.

3.

Realizations:

Notes/Reminders:

Day 51

Date:

Take 3 minutes and look around the kitchen. Be on the lookout for: food in the fridge

What don't you like?

What 3 things can you throw out, donate, regift and get rid of?

1.

2.

3.

Realizations:

Notes/Reminders:

Day 52

Date:

Take 3 minutes and look around your online accounts.

Be on the lookout for: Friends you Follow

What "friends" show up in your newsfeed who you don't really need to follow?

What 3 "relationships" can you let go of?

1.

2.

3.

Realizations:

Notes/Reminders:

Day 53

Date:

Take 3 minutes and look around the bathroom. Be on the lookout for: make up

It's almost gone.. use it up or throw out the rest now!

What 3 things can you throw out, donate, regift and get rid of?

1.

2.

3.

Realizations:

Notes/Reminders:

Day 54

Date:

Take 3 minutes and look around storage areas. Be on the lookout for: old stuff

Maybe stuff from the previous stage of your life is ready to make its exit!

What 3 things can you throw out, donate, regift and get rid of?

1.

2.

3.

Realizations:

Notes/Reminders:

Day 55

Date:

Take 3 minutes and look around the office. Be on the lookout for: office supplies

Let go of those cute, random promotional items.

What 3 things can you throw out, donate, regift and get rid of?

1.

2.

3.

Realizations:

Notes/Reminders:

Day 56

Date:

Take 3 minutes and look around the bathroom. Be on the lookout for: other self care items

Check the drawers, around the space - what else can go?

What 3 things can you throw out, donate, regift and get rid of?

1.

2.

3.

Realizations:

Notes/Reminders:

Day 57

Date:

Take 3 minutes and look around **Wild Card.**

Check around the front door area

Inside and out - how's the first impression?

Anything to get rid of?

What 3 things can you throw out, donate, regift and get rid of?

1.

2.

3.

Realizations:

Notes/Reminders:

Day 58

Date:

Take 3 minutes and look around your devices. Be on the lookout for: photos in your camera roll?

All the rest of the group shots that were taken to choose the 1 good one?
What 3 photos did you delete?

1.

2.

3.

Realizations:

Notes/Reminders:

Day 59

Date:

Take 3 minutes and look around the closet. Be on the lookout for: Loungewear

What did you buy that you thought you would love, but you really don't?

What 3 things can you throw out, donate, regift and get rid of?

1.

2.

3.

Realizations:

Notes/Reminders:

Day 60

Date:

Take 3 minutes and look around the kitchen.
Be on the lookout for: spices

>You bought it for a recipe, once, and haven't opened it since.

What 3 things can you throw out, donate, regift and get rid of?

1.

2.

3.

Realizations:

Notes/Reminders:

Day 61

Date:

Take 3 minutes and look around the kitchen. Be on the lookout for: pantry or shelves

Got a crazy gadget that you never even use?

What 3 things can you throw out, donate, regift and get rid of?

1.

2.

3.

Realizations:

Notes/Reminders:

Day 62

Date:

Take 3 minutes and look around online banking.

Be on the lookout for: subscriptions

What services do you no longer use or want?

What 3 things can you stop paying for?

1.

2.

3.

Realizations:

Notes/Reminders:

Day 63

Date:

Take 3 minutes and look around storage spaces.

Be on the lookout for: stuff for trip packing

    How many toiletry zipper pouches do you really need?

What 3 things can you throw out, donate, regift and get rid of?

1.

2.

3.

Realizations:

Notes/Reminders:

Day 64

Date:

Take 3 minutes and look around storage zones.

Be on the lookout for: celebratory items
- Anything from a holiday you don't really celebrate anymore?

What 3 things can you throw out, donate, regift and get rid of?

1.

2.

3.

Realizations:

Notes/Reminders:

Day 65

Date:

Take 3 minutes and look around the closet. Be on the lookout for: active wear

What doesn't fit right? What de-motivates instead of motivates you to work out? What 3 things can you throw out, donate, regift and get rid of?

1.

2.

3.

Realizations:

Notes/Reminders:

Day 66

Date:

Take 3 minutes and look around **Wild Card.**
Look around!

Any space, any place.. just find 3 items that no longer belong here!
What 3 things can you throw out, donate, regift and get rid of?

1.

2.

3.

Realizations:

Notes/Reminders:

Day 67

Date:

Take 3 minutes and look around the closet. Be on the lookout for: socks

Any ugly socks you just really won't wear?

What 3 things can you throw out, donate, regift and get rid of?

1.

2.

3.

Realizations:

Notes/Reminders:

Day 68

Date:

Take 3 minutes and look around the bathroom. Be on the lookout in the under sink area

Any random items.. that don't even really belong under the bathroom sink? What 3 things can you throw out, donate, regift and get rid of?

1.

2.

3.

Realizations:

Notes/Reminders:

Day 69

Date:

Take 3 minutes and look around the office. Be on the lookout for: paper clutter

Can you shred any bills, notices, & other (once) important documents that no longer are?
What 3 things can you throw out, donate, regift and get rid of?

1.

2.

3.

Realizations:

Notes/Reminders:

Day 70

Date:

Take 3 minutes and look around the closet.
Be on the lookout for: "unmentionables"

C'mon, we all have one thing (or more) that could really go!

What 3 things can you throw out, donate, regift and get rid of?

1.

2.

3.

Realizations:

Notes/Reminders:

Day 71

Date:

Take 3 minutes and look around the office. Be on the lookout for: small electronics

Any cords or wires that you have no idea what they go to?

What 3 things can you throw out, donate, regift and get rid of?

1.

2.

3.

Realizations:

Notes/Reminders:

Day 72

Date:

Take 3 minutes and look around the kitchen. Be on the lookout for: glassware

Do you have a collection of souvenir shot glasses that are ready to move on? What 3 things can you throw out, donate, regift and get rid of?

1.

2.

3.

Realizations:

Notes/Reminders:

Day 73

Date:

Take 3 minutes and look around the closet. Be on the lookout for: jewelry

Got an earring that's missing a mate?
Out-of-style stuff?

What 3 things can you throw out, donate, regift and get rid of?

1.

2.

3.

Realizations:

Notes/Reminders:

Day 74

Date:

Take 3 minutes and look around the office.
Be on the lookout for: Hobby Supplies

Do you have duplicates of any supplies?

What 3 things can you throw out, donate, regift and get rid of?

1.

2.

3.

Realizations:

Notes/Reminders:

Day 75

Date:

Take 3 minutes and look around the closet. Be on the lookout for: shoes

Any special occasion shoes that you won't wear (again)?

What 3 things can you throw out, donate, regift and get rid of?

1.

2.

3.

Realizations:

Notes/Reminders:

Day 76

Date:

Take 3 minutes and look around the office.

Be on the lookout for: books

Guides and resource books that have been replaced by google?

What 3 things can you throw out, donate, regift and get rid of?

1.

2.

3.

Realizations:

Notes/Reminders:

Day 77

Date:

Take 3 minutes and look around the bathroom. Be on the lookout for: towels

Do you NEED all the towels in here?

What 3 things can you throw out, donate, regift and get rid of?

1.

2.

3.

Realizations:

Notes/Reminders:

Day 78

Date:

Take 3 minutes and look around the closet.

Be on the lookout for: accessories

The tiny clutch that's too small to hold your big phone? Something else?

What 3 things can you throw out, donate, regift and get rid of?

1.

2.

3.

Realizations:

Notes/Reminders:

Day 79

Date:

Take 3 minutes and look around your home screen

Be on the lookout for: Apps on your devices

What app is a big time waster and you want it gone for good?

What 3 things can you clear out?

1.

2.

3.

Realizations:

Notes/Reminders:

Day 80

Date:

Take 3 minutes and look around the closet.
Be on the lookout for: appearal

Look for something you bought that you never wore.

What 3 things can you throw out, donate, regift and get rid of?

1.

2.

3.

Realizations:

Notes/Reminders:

Day 81

Date:

Take 3 minutes and look around **Wild Card.**
Be on the lookout for: tchotchkes and ornaments

Are you ready to release some tchotchkes? What 3 things can you throw out, donate, regift and get rid of?

1.

2.

3.

Realizations:

Notes/Reminders:

Day 82

Date:

Take 3 minutes and look around your drives.
Be on the lookout for: Docs Saved on Devices

Any old lists or plans that are finished?
Do you have projects that you never need to open again?
What 3 things can you right click to get rid of?

1.

2.

3.

Realizations:

Notes/Reminders:

Day 83

Date:

Take 3 minutes and look around the kitchen. Be on the lookout inside the drawers

Any broken or damaged pieces?
Anything missing a piece or an attachment?
What 3 things can you throw out, donate, regift and get rid of?

1.

2.

3.

Realizations:

Notes/Reminders:

Day 84

Date:

Take 3 minutes and look around the kitchen.
Be on the lookout for: groceries

What won't you finish.. really?

What 3 things can you throw out, donate, regift and get rid of?

1.

2.

3.

Realizations:

Notes/Reminders:

Day 85

Date:

Take 3 minutes and look around your digital social world.

Be on the lookout for: People on your Feeds

Who you do you always scroll right past?

What 3 people can you delete, block or pause?

1.

2.

3.

Realizations:

Notes/Reminders:

Day 86

Date:

Take 3 minutes and look around the bathroom. Be on the lookout for: cosmetics

Maybe it was a gift - regift it to the garbage!

What 3 things can you throw out, donate, regift and get rid of?

1.

2.

3.

Realizations:

Notes/Reminders:

Day 87

Date:

Take 3 minutes and look around the storage. Be on the lookout for: memories

Maybe now is the time to let go of old cards, pictures, souvenirs?

What 3 things can you throw out, donate, regift and get rid of?

1.

2.

3.

Realizations:

Notes/Reminders:

Day 88

Date:

Take 3 minutes and look around the office.

Be on the lookout for: work accessories

Time to lose extra pads of paper, broken pencils, and the billion paperclips you'll never use.

What 3 things can you throw out, donate, regift and get rid of?

1.

2.

3.

Realizations:

Notes/Reminders:

Day 89

Date:

Take 3 minutes and look around the bathroom. Be on the lookout for: pampering items

Take a look around the space - what else is out?

What 3 things can you throw out, donate, regift and get rid of?

1.

2.

3.

Realizations:

Notes/Reminders:

Day 90

Date:

Take 3 minutes and look around **Wild Card.**

Be on the lookout for: outdoors

Look around outside your space.
What doesn't belong?

What 3 things can you throw out, donate, regift and get rid of?

1.

2.

3.

Realizations:

Notes/Reminders:

Day 91

Date:

Take 3 minutes and look around your devices
Take a scroll through your photo roll.

Do you have any unintentional screenshots or accidental photos that can go?

What 3 things can you images can you delete?

1.

2.

3.

Realizations:

Notes/Reminders:

Day 92

Date:

Take 3 minutes and look around the closet.
Be on the lookout for: comfy clothes

What's just too worn to keep?

What 3 things can you throw out or get rid of?

1.

2.

3.

Realizations:

Notes/Reminders:

Day 93

Date:

Take 3 minutes and look around the kitchen. Be on the lookout for: condiments

Anything expired? Have your tastes changed?

What 3 things can you throw out, donate, regift and get rid of?

1.

2.

3.

Realizations:

Notes/Reminders:

Day 94

Date:

Take 3 minutes and look around the kitchen.
Be on the lookout for: Behind Closed Doors

Got a crazy gadget that you never even use?

What 3 things can you throw out, donate, regift and get rid of?

1.

2.

3.

Realizations:

Notes/Reminders:

Day 95

Date:

Take 3 minutes and look around bank statements.

Be on the lookout for: Daily-Weekly-Monthly

Scan your statement to see what you're paying for monthly that you can pause for now.. or cancel all together - maybe 3 things to save you over $10 a month?! Score!

What 3 things can you cancel?

1.

2.

3.

Realizations:

Notes/Reminders:

Day 96

Date:

Take 3 minutes and look around storage areas. Looks like it's time for taking a trip (to the trash)

    Do you have an inflatable travel pillow that isn't really comfortable?

What 3 things can you throw out, donate, regift and get rid of?

1.

2.

3.

Realizations:

Notes/Reminders:

Day 97

Date:

Take 3 minutes and look around more storage. Be on the lookout for: holiday and seasonal

Any seasonal items that were a good idea at the time, but don't get used that much? Do you have any old Valentine's stuff.. from an old valentine that can go TODAY?

What 3 things can you throw out, donate, regift and get rid of?

1.

2.

3.

Realizations:

Notes/Reminders:

Day 98

Date:

Take 3 minutes and look around the closet.
Be on the lookout for: exercise wear

What did you buy that you thought you would love, but you really don't?

What 3 things can you throw out, donate, regift and get rid of?

1.

2.

3.

Realizations:

Notes/Reminders:

Day 99

Date:

Take 3 minutes and look around **Wild Card.**
Scan your area!

Any space, any place.. just find 3 items that no longer belong here!

What 3 things can you throw out, donate, regift and get rid of?

1.

2.

3.

Realizations:

Notes/Reminders:

*optional: Day 100 - get rid of this notebook.

Congratulations on making it through the last 99 days...
and all that STUFF!

(or - maybe- you flipped back here before you even started the book)

Are you ready for a new notebook or journal? Grab another one of these and/or look for other journals, diaries and notebooks also available.

For example:
-A Daily Gratitude Journal
to notice things you're so appreciative of on a daily basis

-A Dream Interpretation Journal
to train your brain to remember your dreams and figure out their meanings

-A Bright Ideas and Brainstorms Notebook
to collect all your best insights

And so many more!
See them all at bexb.org/shopjournals

Printed in Great Britain
by Amazon